S T I C K M E N ™

S T̈ I C K M E N ™

you always
have to be
in the
headlines,
don't you?

Peter Vegas

**Andrews McMeel
Publishing, LLC**

Kansas City

06 07 08 09 10 BID 10 9 8 7 6 5 4 3 2 1

ISBN-13: 978-0-7407-6210-9
ISBN-10: 0-7407-6210-9

Artwork by Peter Vegas
First published 2004 by Santoro Graphics, London, UK
© 2004 Santoro
All rights reserved

Greeting cards also available from Santoro Graphics Ltd.
UK tel: +44 1709 518 100
www.santorographics.com
For licensing opportunities please contact
licensing@santorographics.com.

I **can't draw horses.** That's how I knew I wasn't good at art. Life is very black and white like that when you're seven. My mate Brendon . . . now he could draw horses! He was really good at drawing them. That meant whenever we had to do a school project, all the girls lined up to get him to draw horses for them. It didn't matter what the topic was, the girls always flocked around Brendon saying, "Brendon, can you draw me a horse on a pyramid?" or "Brendon, draw me a horse realigning the solar panels on the Hubble Telescope."

From my seat at the back of the classroom beside the naughty kid, I sat sulking, bemoaning my lack of artistic talent.

And so it was I came to find some kind of solace in the humble stickman, an uncomplicated bloke for what was a very complicated time of my life. Always willing to spring forth for me from pen, pencil, or charcoal-tipped stick, the stickman was my own simple attempt at artistic expression.

Eventually it was time to fly the education coop, and with drawing skills like mine, it was little wonder that the advertising industry welcomed me with open arms—as a copywriter. After fourteen years of tricking people into buying stuff, I began to toy with the idea of writing a really long, boring book about advertising and target markets and advertising to target markets. But lots of ad people had already done that, and to be honest it seemed a little too much like hard work.

Then out of the ashes of my past, the stickman suddenly reared his circular little head, and before I knew it my black felt-tip pen and I had banged out *Stickmen*—a book that some are saying will go down in history as one of the great literary achievements.*

Originally, I saw this book as the perfect replacement for the 1970s women's magazines that you find in doctors' waiting rooms, or in the cabinet under the TV at Aunt Cathy's house. But after lengthy consultations with a boardroom full of guys named Gary and Dave, far bigger plans have been hatched for this literary masterpiece:

Read the book, have a laugh, and then tell eighteen people to buy it. Our actuaries have calculated that if everyone who reads it tells eighteen people to buy a copy, and they actually do, then within eighteen months there will be a copy of *Stickmen* on every second coffee table and in every fourth toilet in the entire world!

If we all play our part, the stickman will rise like a rising thing made of sticks, and take its rightful place right near the very top of the illustration food pyramid—up high where the air is thin and even the most well-drawn horse finds it so hard to breathe that it doesn't normally survive.

This book is dedicated to all those people who can't draw horses.

Peter Vegas

*To be honest, the only person saying this book will go down as one of the great literary achievements is my mom. But she was right about flared pants coming back in, so ya never know.

S TICKMEN™

Page boy

Tenpin Bowler

Parking warden

A little person? Or someone far away?

tennis player

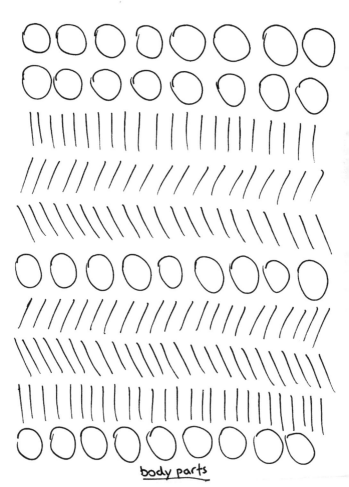

body parts

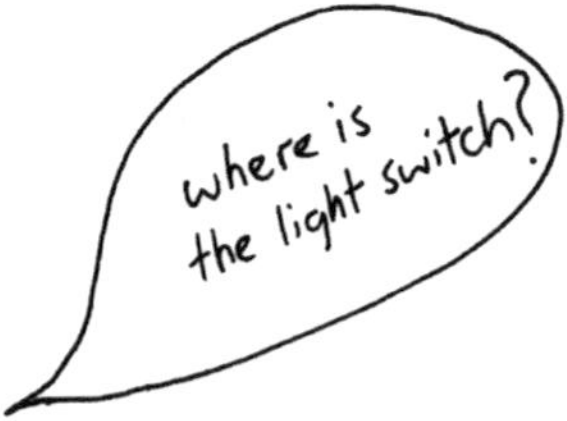
where is the light switch?

stickman

The history of the stickman

The humble stickman can be traced back to the earliest days of man. Long before pen and paper, this simple character was applied to smooth rocky walls with the aid of a sooty twig. Many assume that these primitive drawings were created by our forefathers, but now a group of dodgy-looking scholars in bad-fitting cardigans, who give off the distinct impression that they know exactly what they're talking about, have hypothesized that in actual fact, the earliest stickmen drawings were probably created not by cavemen, but by cave children.

I hate it when they don't leave enough room for the illustrations

The reason behind this stunning revision of popular theory is that in those days cave moms wouldn't let their kids go out and play on account of all the saber-toothed tigers that liked eating little children and woolly mammoths that were so shortsighted they often sat on children after mistaking them for small, smelly, hairy, lumpy cushions. As a result, cave children spent a lot of time in their caves drawing on the walls, which, unlike today, was quite acceptable in even the very flashiest cave dwellings.

Traditionalists are quick to point out that if cave children did spend a lot of time inside, then they probably would have been forced to help with the chores. This theory was refuted by well-known "cave children drew stickmen" advocate Ken Massey. He pointed out that early man's cave dwellings were very maintenance-friendly and it was entirely possible that cave children could have finished their limited chores and still had plenty of time to draw stickmen until Dad came home with fresh wildebeest for dinner.

alien

Lady from Nai Soi

math teacher

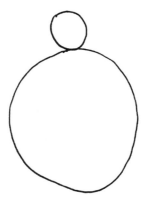

stickman behind tractor wheel

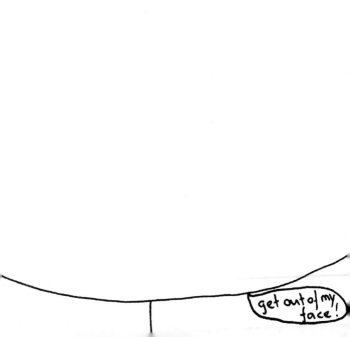

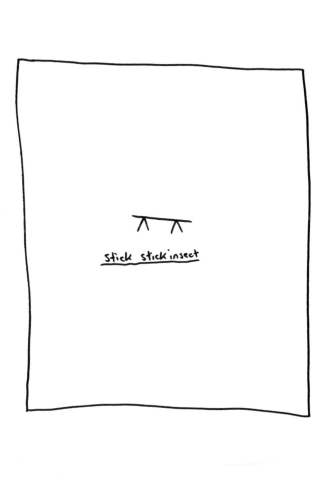

stick stick insect

crop circle expert

on the edge

Pac man man

man of the world

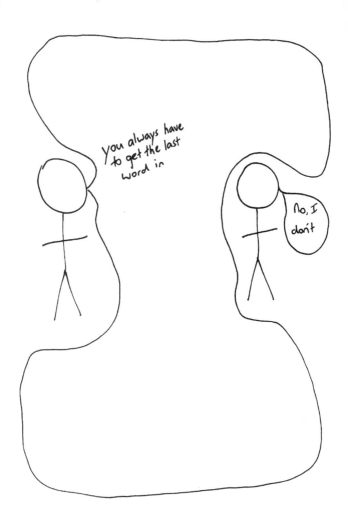

Hermit

Hippie

Sherlock Holmes

Creative type

Strong, silent type

DJ

Olympian

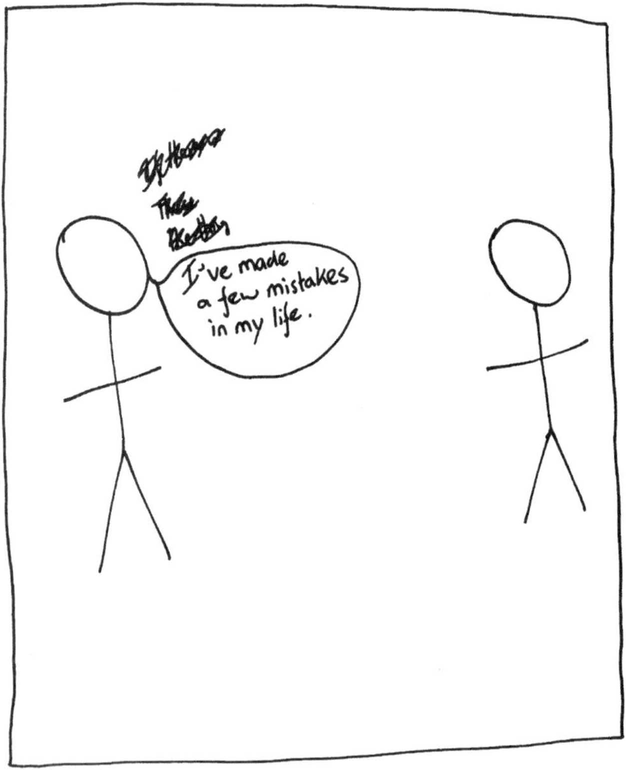
I've made a few mistakes in my life.

Pregnant

smarty pants

Skier

Stickman with a jump rope

Evolution of the stickman

Convict

how stickmen draw stickmen

Booze

Supermodel

Give me a call, I'm in the book

Stickman A L & K B 37 Hamish Pl Espom.................621 789
Stickman B W 5/41 Empire Ave HerBy.................377 246
Stickman C R 85 Jefferries Rd MtWel.................525 678
Stickman E H 134 Harley Ave Hwick................. 412 734
Stickman F S 23 George St Remra.................572 347
Stickman H S 21 Hamish Pl MtEdn.................623 713
Stickman I 64 Spawn Rd Ptchv.................846 731
Stickman I E & T W 6 Rongopai Rd MtRk.................733 897
Stickman J M 16 Metson Ave Hendn.................813 459
Stickman K O & K L 110 Schultz St Rem.................626 783
Stickman L A 52 Montressor Ave NewLn.................824 529
Stickman L B 18 Powesland Ave TataS.................834 649
Stickman M S 69 Flick Street AkCen.................375 932
Stickman N L & K B 37 Teson Rd Espom.................621 789
Stickman O D 723 Maunsell Rd Parnl.................547 246
Stickman O R 87 Ladbrook Rd MtWel.................525 778
Stickman P H 13 Burgham Rd Pknga.................566 892
Stickman P S 41 Nola Ave Remra.................772 347
Stickman R S 21 Monkey Hill MtEdn.................667 713
Stickman SA 34 Venturer St Ptchv.................649 731
Stickman U E & T W 76 Sunnyhills Rd Pknga.................569 897
Stickman VS 361 New North Rd MtEden................. 309 408
Stickman VU 11 Munns St Pknga.................573 493
Stickman W R 12 Massey Rd BlokB.................424 529
Stickman XL 38 Blakey Cre Sndhm.................834 649
Stickman ZS 8 Healy St AkCen.................345 442